Importance of Writing Storie

For weeks after my daughter had been to a fire safety presentation at the elementary school, she slept with her scrapbook instead of the usual teddy bear and dolls. She was told that if there was a fire in the house she had to get out quickly and that everything else had to be left behind. She was sure that if she slept with her scrapbook, then surely she could save it too.

Her scrapbook didn't have fancy layouts or even very many photos. But it did have stories–memories with which she couldn't part.

Today, creating a scrapbook has become a refined art. New and exciting scrapbooking products are enabling parents to create the most elaborate books. Parents everywhere want their children's books to be fun, beautiful and unforgettable. But most of all, they want them to be treasured, much as my daughter treasures hers.

The Art of Writing Scrapbook Stories© introduces a new dimension in scrapbooking. This book shows how to make your scrapbooks memorable by combining stories with pictures. Scrapbooks which include stories are a beginning of a child's history and will teach her that what she said and did is as important as how she looked. The photographs will catch the attention of a child, but the stories will make the visual images significant.

Photograph by JayLynn Studios, Inc.

Lucy Armstrong, Janice Dixon and Suzanne Dixon

This book shows you how to capture the moments of your child's life–loving stories about your children–stories that are interesting, fun and often told in your child's own words.

Sounds difficult? It isn't! Most of the stories in this book were taken from letters to friends and family. In this book, I will take you step-by-step through a simplified writing process and show you how easy and enjoyable it can be.

My daughter (yes, the same one), Lucy Armstrong, and my daughter-in-law, Suzanne Dixon, have joined with me to present ideas on how to collect, write and present a scrapbook that your children will love, enjoy and want to read again and again.

Janice Dixon

Note: Names and dates have been changed throughout this book for reasons of privacy.

Acknowledgements

We would like to thank the many people who have helped in the writing, planning and printing of this book. The companies who have worked with us have been wonderful, and we appreciate their assistance and usage of their products.

Stacy Julian and Terina Darcy of Core Composition steered us in the right direction. D.J. Inkers and D.O.T.S Design Studio created some of our layout designs. Barbara Williams, Peg Nichols, and Sally Taylor helped with the editing. Others have shared their talents, such as Portia Mandel of Memorybook Lane, Terri Carter of Pebbles in my Pocket, and Brent Budd of S.L. Community College.

We also appreciate those who waited anxiously for this book. Your interest has encouraged us throughout the development process.

Scrapbook Writing is Easy

Writing scrapbook stories is not only important, it is easy. On the cover of this book is a story of my granddaughter, Brianna. We were scrubbing the floor and she handed me the mop rag and said, "Choke it for me, Grandma." I did not immediately run to my computer and type up this story, but I did grab a pencil to write the punch line on a sheet of paper. I embellished details later. Writing five words is not overwhelming. You can write down punch lines.

Whenever your child says or does something wonderful, write it down. Include date, place, child. The sentences don't have to be complete. Grab the moment, write down the basics and put the paper aside to work on later. Then when you do have more time, the information is there for you.

Put your child's sayings in her file, folder, or photo safe box, along with her drawings, photographs, report cards, and mementos.

One way to collect stories is to write a letter to a family member or friend. Devote one paragraph about each child. Copy the letter and use that paragraph in the child's scrapbook. I had six children, six scrapbooks and one letter monthly from which to draw.

If you keep a journal, include a paragraph about each child. Express your feelings. Stories can be taken right from your journal or entries may just be used to trigger memories of a story you may want to write.

If you have a busy schedule, consider thinking about your stories as you do the dishes, wait in store lines, run errands, etc. When you eventually sit down to write, the stories will come more readily because you've already created them in your mind.

When you're ready to start your scrapbook page(s), take a look to see if there are stories and photos that will go together.

When Willard and I returned from Hawaii, we brought hula costumes for our granddaughters. The girls had to try them right on.

Louise looked over at Diane and complained, "Her coconuts are bigger than mine."

DIANE

LOUISE

The girls performing "Tiny Bubbles"
May 1992

Page Layout Tips

Decide how you would like to organize your scrapbooks. You can focus on each child separately, make a family scrapbook, or follow a theme such as holidays, vacations etc.

Once these organizing decisions have been made, document and separate your pictures and mementos; then place them into acid-free boxes or files.

Credits: stationery by Sonburn, Inc., photograph by JayLynn Studios, Inc., wave paper edgers by Fiskars®, fish & palm tree small punches by Family Treasures, heart punch by McGill, twirl font by DJ Inkers

Writing Tips

Not every layout page has to have a story. Writing this many stories could be overwhelming. Add them as often as you can.

The Art of Writing Scrapbook Stories©

October 11, 1963

Lucy is no longer going to nursery school. She flunked naptime.

Handwriting and Computers

When my mother was a girl, handwriting was a practiced art. Her handwriting was beautiful and easy to read. She wrote many personal remembrances in her own hand, and I value her penmanship almost as much as I value her words.

When I was a girl, the art of penmanship was still highly valued, and I remember spending countless hours trying to make perfect circles. I hated the monotony of that wasted motion! After all that practicing, my handwriting wasn't any better.

Some people don't like their handwriting and prefer to type everything. Others like to type because it's quick, easy and readable.

One woman told me that when she was twelve years old, her mother died and the only thing she had with her mother's handwriting was a grocery list. She treasures that scrap of paper.

Your handwriting should be in your child's scrapbook, but you must choose when and where it is appropriate. Be sure to have your child and other family members handwrite in her scrapbook.

Personal stories, such as a mother sharing her feelings about the birth of her new son (see page 14), could be handwritten.

Stories which are short in length, documentation and phrases are excellent places to show your handwriting.

However, you don't have to handwrite everything. Longer stories are easier to read and fit better on a page if you type the story, as we have done on many pages in this book. I find that when I type my stories, even the shorter ones, the stories are read more often.

Stories can be printed directly onto stationery paper or can be cut and pasted. Use whichever method works for you. It is a good idea is to get these pages done so your children can enjoy them while they are growing up.

Credits: stationery by Sonburn, Inc., paper punches by McGill, ripple paper edgers by Fiskars®, pen by Zig® Memory System® Writer

Writing Tips

As you write your stories, place them with photos that occurred near the same time frame. But don't worry if the photos and stories don't match. Remember, many wonderful stories happen when a photographer isn't around.

Page Layout Tips

If you are handwriting your story, place a lined piece of paper behind the page you are working on to give you a guide to follow. If you can't see the lines underneath, hold the paper up to a window or use a light table.

Another method is to draw light lines with a #2 mechanical pencil. Write your story with an approved archival pen, then erase the pencil lines after the ink dries. Be sure to use a white eraser that can be purchased from art or office supply stores.

•Docu-tell •Quick-tell •Photo-tell • Story-tell

You can write a little or a lot in your scrapbook. The important thing is to write something. Without words, you leave your viewer in a silent world.

There are four degrees of scrapbook writing. I have divided them into docu-tell, quick-tell, photo-tell and story-tell.

Docu-telling indicates who is in the picture, when the photo was taken and where. A neighbor child asked, "Mama, who is that person in the picture? "I don't know," her mother replied. "You tell me who it is and from now on that's who it will be." Obviously this mom waited too long to docu-tell her photos. Always docu-tell your photos and page layouts. The docu-tell of this layout is found in the upper left corner and along the side.

Quick-telling includes single word exclamations and short word phrases such as "wow!" An example of quick-telling is included on page 19. These words add life to the page and are fun to read, but are not required.

Photo-telling (sometimes called photo-journaling) is additional material about the photo. This is used to tell what was happening in the picture. The photo-telling on this layout reveals the mood JaNae was in when her picture was being taken. Photo-telling is used when a story is caught on camera or when additional information helps the reader understand more about the photo.

Story-telling includes experiences or memories that let you know more about your child's personality. Just as you keep a camera available to take pictures, also keep a notebook handy, ready to record your child's words and actions.

Sometimes you may have a story, but you don't have a photo to accompany the event. A posed photo works well in this circumstance.

Story by story, the experiences of a child's life join together to become the beginning of her written life history.

Page Layout Tips

Computers help make scrapbooking fast, easy and versatile.

On a computer, you are able to import clip art and change its size to fit your needs. You can then rotate your image and flip it vertically or horizontally. Layering objects on top of one another, such as in this design, is another option.

If you have a color printer, print your design in color. If not, print the design in black and white and then hand color your page.

Credits: stationery by Memory Press, computer clip art by Homespun Software™, jumbo lace scallop paper craft scissors by Family Treasures, photograph by Olan Mills

Writing Tips

Are you confused about where to start? Consider writing about the following:
- Her birth
- Things she says
- Humorous events
- Achievements
- Changes in her life

The Art of Writing Scrapbook Stories©

JARON

Jaron is seven years old and excited to be getting birthday presents. He has told his friends about his party and, of course, invited them all. One little boy couldn't come, but Jaron said, "That's all right. You can send the present tomorrow." We had a nice long discussion on etiquette.

August 8, 1995

HAPPY BIRTHDAY

GARRETT
COURTNEY
JARON
JENNER
KIRSTEN
DERRICK
RAEANNE
JANAE

7

CENTERVILLE, UT.

Credits: deckle edge scissors by Family Treasures, pinking & bubbles paper edgers by Fiskars®, balloon & star punch by McGill, lettering idea by "ABC's of Creative Lettering", EK Success, picket font by DJ Inkers

Page Layout Tips

When using patterned scissors or edgers, line up each cut with the last cut so that the pattern is not broken.

Save your scraps and use them for decorations, punches and small shapes.

Organize your scraps by placing them in files, envelopes, or individual boxes. For example, all different shades of red scraps may go into your "red file"

Writing Tips

Birthdays are a great time to record height, weight, likes, dislikes, goals, dreams, etc. These can be fun to compare from year to year. Ask your child about his favorite activities, friends and foods.

Find Your Story Idea

Everything in your story is going to revolve around one key idea. You can take a general subject, such as a birthday party, first day of school, moving from one house to another, or visiting grandma. The subject doesn't have to be world shattering. Common, everyday subjects are sometimes best.

Now that you have a general idea, try to decide what was the most important part of that subject. When your child went to school the first time, what was the part that stood out most? (Was he confident, excited or frightened? Did he howl all the way to school?)

This key idea is usually included in your first sentence and is an introduction of your idea to your reader.

The introduction sets your direction and includes:
1. The child's name (Jaron)
2. What is happening (a birthday party)
3. Your key idea (excited about getting presents)

Jaron is having a birthday party. Again, what was the best part of his party? Is it the games, the children, the refreshments, or the presents? Decide on one thing that made this birthday memorable. Typically for many children, and in Jaron's case, it was the anticipation of getting all the presents.

Everything in the story is going to revolve around this idea. As you write your story, don't let other ideas creep into your story. Don't talk about blowing up the balloons, or baking a cake. Focus on Jaron's excitement in receiving gifts from his friends.

Most key ideas are only one sentence, but they can be longer. When you are finished with the story, go back and make sure that everything refers to these first few sentences. Make sure you name the child, tell what is happening, and focus on the key idea.

Develop Your Story

The first sentence introduces the subject and indicates who is involved. The last sentence summarizes and finishes the story. But most of the writing develops the story idea.

The development of a story includes action. One action leads to the next. Action can include:
- physical activity
- conversation
- ideas

When you use physical action, something must happen to make the story move from starting point to final conclusion. When the story is being told, there should be a feeling of progression from one activity to another. If you are going to tell about taking a child fishing, first give the theme sentence, which is: On Saturday I took Josh fishing for the first time.

Now tell what happened: We dug worms, drove to my favorite fishing hole, put a worm on the hook and waited for the fish to bite. This shows Josh and you in action. You are progressing from one activity to the next, all in preparation for catching the fish.

When using conversation, you need to go somewhere in that dialogue. It isn't enough to simply let the person talk. There needs to be purpose in the conversation. In this case, Mark is trying to keep a secret and everything he says lets you know that keeping his secret is going to be the most difficult thing he does. This is dialogue action.

Ideas also must progress so that when you have finished, the idea has been clarified, developed, enhanced, or changed. Usually this takes place when you are writing an essay using such subjects as consideration, love, unselfishness, knowledge, etc.

Development of your story will be discussed further throughout the book, especially in the section on "Give Examples, page 8."

Mark is making me a wonderful Christmas present in school, but I'm not sure he can sustain the suspense of keeping a secret.

"It's going to be a surprise, momma," he told me. "And I won't ever tell."

"I won't ask you what it is then," I assured him.

"You are really going to like it, but you can't ask me what it is, because it's a surprise."

"It's going to be difficult, Mark, but I won't ask you."

"You can't guess, can you, mama?"

"No, I can't guess."

Mark looked around the room to see if anyone else was in the room, then leaned over to me and whispered, "Do you want a hint?"

Christmas 1968

To Mom

The Secret

Decorative Designs© & ™Ellison. Licensed Product

Page Layout Tips

In this book, many of our designs are single page layouts with only one picture. We did this because we were limited in space.

In your own books, you may want to consider extending your designs to double page layouts using several more photos and die cuts. This will help keep your pages from clashing with each other.

Credits: holiday & white dots on green paper by The Paper Patch, die cuts by Ellison, deckle edge scissors by Family Treasures, holly days and crayon fonts by DJ Inkers

Writing Tips

It is important to write your stories. Children want to know what they said and did. **A poorly written story is better than an unwritten story.** Each time you write, your stories will improve and you will feel more comfortable in your writing.

The Art of Writing Scrapbook Stories©

Conclude Your Story

The first sentence includes the subject of your story. We know that the story is going to be about our Vietnamese refugee and our son, Dan. The second and third paragraphs develop your idea and the last paragraph concludes your story. The final sentence or paragraph can be written in several ways:

- A summary of what has happened
- Dialogue or punch line
- A comment on the situation
- An analysis
- A word of praise
- An expression of your feelings

You can conclude your story many ways, but there is usually a best ending for each story. Consider each of the suggested conclusions listed above.

In this story I chose the punch line ending. Actually, it was the last line that inspired the story. Sometimes you have an idea of how a story is going to flow before you ever start. If you have a humorous story, work toward the last line for the ending.

Summary endings are used to tie up loose ends or show resolution to a problem within the story. This type of conclusion also provides finality to unanswered questions.

A comment might include a hindsight overview. This can be from right after an incident or many years later. Write your story with honesty and then add your editorial comments. Tell how you feel about what happened. This is the time you can display your wit or wisdom.

An analysis can follow an experience the child has had or a repeated action. Tell how he has learned, discovered, understood, or mastered some skill.

Express a word of praise or of feeling. After you tell what the child has accomplished, express your delight that he is doing so well. Be specific in your praise.

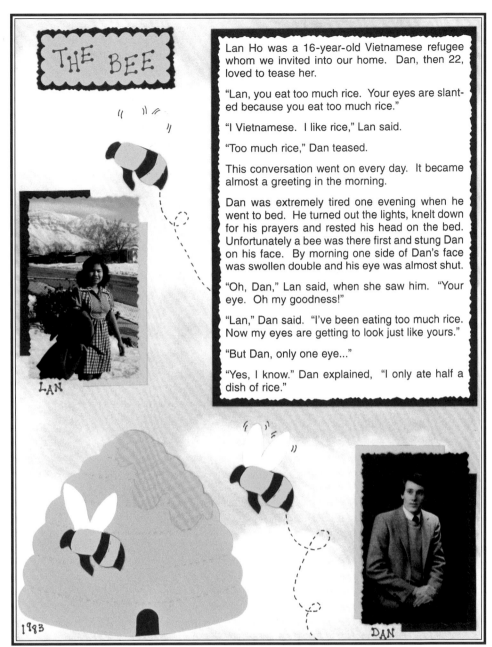

THE BEE

Lan Ho was a 16-year-old Vietnamese refugee whom we invited into our home. Dan, then 22, loved to tease her.

"Lan, you eat too much rice. Your eyes are slanted because you eat too much rice."

"I Vietnamese. I like rice," Lan said.

"Too much rice," Dan teased.

This conversation went on every day. It became almost a greeting in the morning.

Dan was extremely tired one evening when he went to bed. He turned out the lights, knelt down for his prayers and rested his head on the bed. Unfortunately a bee was there first and stung Dan on his face. By morning one side of Dan's face was swollen double and his eye was almost shut.

"Oh, Dan," Lan said, when she saw him. "Your eye. Oh my goodness!"

"Lan," Dan said. "I've been eating too much rice. Now my eyes are getting to look just like yours."

"But Dan, only one eye..."

"Yes, I know." Dan explained, "I only ate half a dish of rice."

LAN

1983

DAN

Credits: cloud stationery by Creative Card Co., deckle edge scissors by Family Treasures, scallop paper edgers & paper crimper by Fiskars®, die cuts by Ellison, layering idea by Terri Carter, photo by JayLynn Studios, Inc.

Page Layout Tips

Remember, your children will grow up and want to take their scrapbooks with them. Consider getting double-prints when you have your film developed, then make a scrapbook for each child and keep the other photos for yourself.

When you purchase your scrapbooking supplies, buy a little extra for your family album.

Writing Tips

If you have recorded the funny things your child has said, then you have your ending already written. Now set the scene and build up to your punch line.

Give Examples

One way to develop your story is to give examples. In this case, I say that the junior matchmakers need to find a groom for Lucy, then I spend a paragraph checking out neighborhood kids for a potential prospect. Choose a story idea, make a statement and then add the words, "for example," in your mind. You don't have to write the words, just use them as a crutch. Lucy is getting married if only local matchmakers can find a groom. For example, they chose Mark, but he sucked his thumb. Lucy is getting married and the neighbor girls are dolling up the bride. For example, they found her a long white dress and a silk baby blanket for a veil.

Your writing will be stronger if you can substantiate it. If you say that Henry is lazy, Wilber is ambitious or Ryan is doing well in school, be sure you give examples. When you say that Cody excels in astronomy, then report what he said about the stars and planets, the reader will be convinced.

Examples also make your writing more interesting. I read one story about a swimming party in which the mother told about the balloons and refreshments and, as an afterthought, added, "Everyone had a wonderful time except that Suzy nearly drowned."

This story left me wanting to know what had happened. I didn't care about the balloons, or even the refreshments. The mother was trying to say so much about the party that she forgot to focus on Suzie's near brush with death. The mother should have cut the boring stuff and zeroed in on the high action drama.

She should have written, "The children were all diving into the pool for pennies and Suzie got kicked in the head. I guess she took in water and choked. Uncle Bill saw her face down on the bottom of the pool and pulled her out. Susie coughed three times and started to breath again. Luckily she had only been under water a short time and is fine now."

Right now Lucy is getting married, if they can find a groom.

All day long Katie, 11, and Becky, 8, have been dolling Lucy up. They found her a long white dress and a silk baby blanket for a veil. They put her hair up in curlers and made her a crown.

The only thing left was finding a bridegroom. They were going to choose Mark, but he sucked his thumb. Then they decided that Kyle, 7, was just the right age for my little five-year-old, but Kyle ran too fast. So they compromised on four-year-old Russell. They carried him to the wedding, but he was frightened at being the center of attention and started howling. Robert also refused the honor because he was baking a devil's food cake for the reception and Danny was too wet from running through the sprinklers with his clothes on.

So we had the reception anyway and Lucy was left at the altar without a groom.

Page Layout Tips

On this page we typed the story directly onto the stationery, then added the photo and decorations.

If you have a font that ties into the theme, use it, but be careful not to go overboard on font choices. Too many fonts or font sizes on one page can be distracting.

Credits: stationery by ©Frances Meyer, Inc.®, heart die cut by Accu-Cut Systems®, pen by Uchida, wedding cut outs by ScrapEase

Writing Tips

If you find yourself telling your neighbor about the "darling thing" your child said or did, then it's time to start writing. As adults, our own actions can become repetitive, but your child is creating and experimenting with new ideas and actions every day. Write about her imaginative playtime.

The Art of Writing Scrapbook Stories©

Robert Won't Sing

Robert's report card wasn't too bad except for music. He refuses to sing. Absolutely not one note. This baffles his poor teacher who thinks all children should love to sing. November 1963

Keep It Simple

A story doesn't have to be long to be effective. Sometimes a simple sentence or two is all you need. Other times, a much longer story is necessary to express what you need to say.

I could have discussed why Robert wouldn't sing, but I honestly didn't know. I was only aware of the teacher's frustration. The content of this story is slight, so there is no reason to stretch the length.

Simple writing often comes from your letters to friends or family. Have fun in your writing. Pretend that you are on the phone telling family members about your child's escapades, frustrations, and triumphs.

Write about the simple things in your child's life. Tell about the games he plays. Does he lean into his curves as he cruises past the kitchen counter at full speed? Does your child fake illnesses to get out of school? Describe his best theatrical tummy-ache. Tell how your child makes his bed. Is he methodical or does he throw his sheets and blankets all together? These things may not seem important now, but as he grows up, he will delight in knowing about his character traits when he was younger.

When you have your story and outline in mind, start writing. Don't worry about anything except getting words down on paper. Don't let an editor or English teacher sit on your shoulder and criticize. Just write.

You will find that often it takes a sentence or two to get started. Use these sentences until you're comfortable. When you get to the point you wanted to make, write without worrying about grammar, writing style or punctuation. **It is easier to edit than to create.**

After you have written your story, go back and take out unnecessary words or sentences. Edit your story using an underliner pen. This way you can see what you have deleted. Read what you have written both ways and choose the best version.

Credits: paper by Memory Press, dragon back paper edgers by Fiskars®, clip art and doodlers font by DJ Inkers

Page Layout Tips

If you want to save money on your background papers, cut out the border and then use the leftover scrap for framing photos, stories and other elements. For example, we only used one sheet of red and white checked paper to complete this page layout.

Clip art can also be economical because you can use your clip art and fonts repeatedly.

Writing Tips

Get into the habit of writing a letter or journal entry regularly so that the memories won't be lost. Use these comments in your scrapbooks "as is" or polish and improve them when you have time.

Be Clear and Precise

Be clear and precise in your writing. Many beginning writers forget to write as they speak. They find themselves using unnatural language in an attempt to impress others. Their writing becomes a smorgasbord of flowery words and complicated concepts.

Sometimes just writing a straightforward story is best. As stated earlier, set the story up with your main idea, develop it, and then conclude your writing. There should be no need to explain your story further.

Often we are afraid that people aren't going to understand what we have written, so we repeat the main point or explain our writing in unnecessary and boring detail. Write so that explanations are unnecessary. If I had explained the story about Bryant and Brianna, the punch line would have been ruined. For instance, this is how my layout story might have read, "Poor Bryant wasn't used to all the walking around and going from store to store. His little legs got so tired, he couldn't go on any more." This isn't needed. Bryant's own words tell his story.

Precision in writing also means that you choose the best word for the story. A thesaurus offers alternative word choices for more effective writing.

Be specific. Say, "Robert had the chickenpox," instead of, "Robert was sick." Say, "Sarah likes to read Dr. Seuss books, especially **Hop on Pop**," instead of, "Sarah likes to read."

Don't be wordy. Sometimes one word will take the place of several, such as "burned" instead of "destroyed by fire," "today" instead of "in this day and age." Make sure each word is necessary.

When you have completed your story, put it aside for awhile. When you come back, re-read what you have written. Does your story say what you intended?

Credits: paper by The Paper Patch, stickers by Provo Craft, mini-pinking paper edgers by Fiskars®, doodlers font by DJ Inkers

Page Layout Tips

Your can create these bags for your own layouts by cutting out squares and rectangles from a variety of patterned paper. Trim the top of the shapes using a pinking scissor/edger.

Twine or string can then be placed behind the paper to look like handles. Add stickers, tissue, confetti or crimped paper to decorate the bags.

Writing Tips

Try to make your language as natural as possible. To do this, use contractions such as: don't, can't I'm, you're, or won't. If your child has a different way of speaking, try to capture those words. For additional examples of using a child's own words, see the grasshopper story on page 21.

Look for Tangents

Look at your beginning sentence. Have you stayed on the subject, or have you taken off on side-trips or tangents? Tangents are extra comments or details that take you away from the original story. The question in all writing is to know how much to put in and what to take out. Ask yourself, "Does this example or detail improve my story?" If it adds, leave it in. If it distracts, take it out.

Most writers outline the direction they want to go before they begin writing. This keeps them from adding unimportant ideas.

Following are some tangents that could have detracted from the story of "Time With Eric." "Eric doesn't like to go to bed at all, and maybe this is because he is a little bit afraid of the dark. He is worried about ghosts in the closet and noises coming from outside. Often I lie down by Eric to settle him. So when he asked me to lie down, I said, "Wait a short minute," because I wanted to finish putting in a load of wash and do the dishes. And besides, I didn't want to stop what I was doing to lie down by a squirmy six-year-old. Have you ever tried to rest when a little boy kicks and wiggles every minute? And Eric is no exception. I think he excels in wiggle-time. But Eric reminded me, "How come you give me the short minutes and you take the long minutes?""

Tangents included:
- Eric's fears
- My household chores
- A discussion on squirmies

Pare your writing to the main subject. A story should be just long enough to cover what happened. Remember to stay on the subject. Anything that distracts from your main purpose of the story should be avoided.

Credits: clock stationery by The Paper Company, patterned paper by Provo Craft, squared font by DJ Inkers, zipper & stamp paper edgers by Fiskars®

Page Layout Tips

Have one nice studio or school picture taken yearly and then take lots of unposed snapshots. Invest in a good 35mm camera and keep it loaded and available for those moments "too cute" to lose.

Most of your snapshots will need to be trimmed. Don't be afraid to crop out unnecessary scenery shots and clutter.

Writing Tips

Don't worry about getting an entire book finished all at once. This is overwhelming. Tell a single story and concentrate on what you want to say about one idea. Take your time. You have a whole scrapbook to introduce your child.

Add Details

Add details to your story. Details are word pictures that help your reader see what you want him to see. Observe your child. Watch what he does and include these items in your writing. You want to allow your reader to observe the same things you did.

When you say, "I was bitten by a dog," the reader is going to think about a dog that he knows, maybe his neighbor's dog which is a trained German Shepherd watchdog. However, when you said dog, you really meant a poodle puppy. Personally, I would rather be bitten by a puppy than a watchdog.

Choose your words carefully. The word "cereal" isn't as effective as "Wheaties." "Three peanut butter sandwiches" is more descriptive than "snack." "Glass of milk" gives a better image than "drink." When you write your stories, use details instead of generalities.

However, don't just throw in the details. Sprinkle them carefully and make sure that they advance your story.

Generalities	Specifics
pet	Siamese kitten
drink	orange juice
clothes	Levis, torn at the knee
hair	long blonde curls
dessert	apple pie

If I had written in generalities, I would have said: "Nothing seems to fill Charles up. He is always eating." Although the above is correct, the details of what he ate give a more accurate account of what happened and are more interesting.

Extraneous details should not be added. For example, I could have said, "Charles got out a Cub Scout pocket knife from his pocket and wiped it on the dishcloth before he spread peanut butter on his three peanut butter sandwiches." This is extraneous because I am deviating from what he is eating to how he is preparing the sandwiches.

Today, Charles ate three peanut butter sandwiches, two oranges, a bowl of Wheaties, a glass of milk, a handful of chocolate chips, a gob of butter and a spoonful of Cherry Jello mix. This tided him over until supper...half an hour later.

February 1966

Used with permission of MM's Designs

Credits: picnic stationery by MM's Designs, blue w/red heart paper by The Paper Patch, die cuts by Accu-Cut Systems®, corner rounder punch by Family Treasures, pinking paper edgers by Fiskars®,

Page Layout Tips

Use patterned, textured and solid papers to add variety to your layouts. Layer these papers under your photos and stories.

Use stationery and papers that compliment the photograph. On this layout, we didn't have color in the photo but we did have the plaid design of Charles' shirt with which to work.

Writing Tips

Get into the habit of observation. What did your child wear to school this morning? Did the shirt he was wearing have a grease spot on the front? Were all the buttons fastened correctly?

Making Rootbeer

Recently, I was teaching my grandson, Ryan, how to make homemade root beer.

"Get out my canner and put in 9 cups of sugar," I directed. Ryan put in about two cups of sugar but needed more. "Run downstairs to the storage buckets and bring me some more sugar," I requested.

I watched as he mixed the sugar, water, yeast and root beer extract together. The sweet fragrance brought back memories from my childhood.

"This doesn't taste very good, Grandma," he complained.

"That's because it doesn't have any fizz," I told him. "You have to wait five days for the yeast to start working." We filled and capped the bottles and put them in a warm spot.

Five days later, we gathered around as Ryan opened the first bottle. The cap popped loudly and pop fizzed all over the counter. We poured a glass and waited for the moment Ryan would taste his first glass of homemade root beer. He sipped it then spit it out. "Yuk!"

"Ryan," I protested. "Don't be so picky. You're just not used to the yeast. Here, let me have a swallow."

Gag! It was awful. Ryan had used salt instead of sugar.

Oct. '97

Ryan

Credits: Background Texture paper and My Legacy Writer™ by Close to My Heart™, stamps by D.O.T.S™, jumbo pinking scissors by Family Treasures, markers by Tombow®, layout by D.O.T.S Design Studio

Page Layout Tips

Be sure to keep your page layouts age and gender appropriate. For instance, older boys would not be comfortable with juvenile designs or feminine pastel colors.

Girl's pages seem to have more options. Their pages can include light pastels, bright colors or even earth tones. The subject determines the colors more than the gender.

Writing Tips

You don't have to write each story chronologically. Try working on recent stories and page layouts first and then remember earlier times. If your child says something today, write it today. However, as you recall old stories, write down what you remember before they are forgotten again.

Use the Senses

When I was nine years old, Mama decided I was not going to be healthy unless I swallowed a tablespoon of cod-liver oil every day. I hid when I smelled the odor of fish wafting through the room. I gagged as the slimy oil went down my throat and tried to wash the aftertaste of fish-oil down with glasses of water. The taste lasted all day long, even after I ate other food.

Some stories lend themselves to writing about the senses more than others. Try to catch yourself in a memory moment. Close your eyes and remember the odors, the sounds, and the tastes. Write them down. Underline the senses when you finish. Have you caught the moment?

Did your child spread jam all over the kitchen? The sweet strawberry smell and the gooey feel is there, as well as the mess. Did your child pour sand in your shoes? How did it feel? Close your eyes and remember.

As you write specifics, be aware that sight is not the only sense you can use. Although you may not think about the other senses, what would life be without the smell of pine trees or onions cooking on the stove?

Not every story needs to include every sense. Each story may require a separate sense to be emphasized.

The smell of yeast and root beer add to my story as does the sound of the cap popping off a bottle of root beer. However, in this story, taste is the target sense. The difference between the taste of salt and sugar is paramount to the conclusion.

Adding sensory images will strengthen your writing. Don't take the senses of hearing, smell, touch, taste and sight for granted in your writing.

When you add the smell of hamburgers cooking on the grill, the touch of silk to your skin, the taste of butter brickle ice cream, or the sound of a yapping dog, it helps your child remember the experiences as they happened.

Share Your Feelings

An older movie actress once said." I never laugh or cry because it would wrinkle my face." When I heard her words, I thought, what an unhappy life that would be for me if I never showed any emotion. I become closer to a person when I laugh or cry with him.

We have all kinds of feelings. We are embarrassed, frustrated, happy, sad—the whole gamut of emotions.

Life isn't always easy. Sometimes a parent, grandparent, sibling, friend or pet dies. Take the time to discuss and write about sad feelings. Focus on the times you spent with them.

Love is also a powerful emotion. Let your child know that you love him. You can never say, "I love you," too many times. Put these feelings in writing.

Write the words, "I am happy when you are gentle with the dog"....or "I'm pleased that you are kind to your friends"...or "proud that you are my son," "I love the way you smile," (or act, clean your room, try hard in school). The list can go on. Sure, you praise him all the time, but somehow, when you write the words, they become credible.

Make a statement, then find an example to demonstrate that feeling. Maybe you watched your child and his friend playing. Jeff got stung by a bee and your son reassured him that he wouldn't tell anyone if he cried.

This example could also be written like this, "Yesterday, when Jeff got stung, I felt terrible. But then, you went over to him and asked, "Are you okay?" You didn't laugh at him or make him feel bad. You knew just what to do. I love you. You are one great kid!"

It's a simple story, but it shows your son that you are proud when he is kind to others.

Laugh with your child, cry with him, talk with him, praise him, write his stories. Let him know that you care.

Decorative Designs© & ™Ellison. Licensed Product

Dear Diary,   May 5, 1991
It's finally over with and tonight I feel fine. I'll be going home tomorrow. I think we will name this boy, Justin Wesley. He is so small, only 6 pounds 10 ounces, and it is hard to imagine taking care of such a little one. Right now one side of his nose is flattened and it looks like he just finished a prize fight! He has lots of black hair all over his head and a little round face. I've quite fallen in love with the little fellow.

It's A Boy!

Mom
Justin

Credits: stationery & sticker by ©Frances Meyer, Inc.®, die cuts by Ellison, filmstrip border punch & teardrop corner lace edge punch by Family Treasures, heart punch by McGill, stamp paper edgers by Fiskars®, photograph by Olan Mills, pen by Zig® Memory System® Writer

Page Layout Tips

Save memorabilia such as cards, announcements, certificates, and hand/foot prints. These can be used as background decorations or they can be your focal point. It depends on their importance.

Check to see if these items are acid-free using a pH testing pen. If they aren't acid-free, make color copies or deacidify them.

If mementos are large, consider having them reduced in size when you make copies.

Writing Tips

Emotional times in your life come when your life is dramatically changed, such as in marriage, birth, death, divorce, etc. Express your feelings when you write about these experiences.

Show Action

You can tell a story or you can show it. Telling a story is like reading a newspaper. The story is there, but you are looking at it from a distance. Showing a story is more like watching television. You go inside the room, watch people move, hear them talk, and see their reactions.

To show a story, add the elements of action, reaction and dialogue. Is the child tearing open presents, crawling after his brother, balancing a screwdriver on his nose, or screaming at the top of his lungs? Let us see and hear him.

You must be in the same room as the child. Invite your readers in and let them see for themselves that the child is alive. Let the child yawn, jump up and down, or become impatient. Let us feel his emotions.

Why is the child whining? What does he say? Use short sentences like, "Mom, Eric's bothering me!" or "I can do it myself!" and exclamations like "Hurry," or "Wow!" Let us hear him.

I originally wrote this as a "telling" story. It sounded like this:

Robert is building child-sized cars with the "Erector" set we gave him for Christmas this year. The pieces of the set are exactly the right size to build cars big enough for three-year-old Mark to ride. So, Robert makes a car and away Mark rides. In the midst of Mark's joy, Robert decides that a jeep might be a better toy. The whole toy is dismantled to the sound of Mark's wails.

Read the story in the layout and you can see a difference. The story is more fun because it takes you where the action is. You can see Robert and Mark move and hear them speak.

You probably don't want to show every story using action and dialogue, but you will find that many stories are better if you "show" your stories, rather than "tell" them.

Robert and Mark

Dec. 1966 at our Montclair Home SLC, UT.

Robert was so excited when he saw his new *Erector* set under the Christmas tree. It had super-sized pieces, with four large wheels.

"I can make a real car!" he exclaimed.

Three-year-old Mark could hardly wait. He wasn't interested in his own blocks and firetruck. "Hurry!" he told Robert. "I wanna ride!"

I bet I can make a car or jeep with this set," Robert decided. "Wow!"

Mark kept getting in the way, trying to see everything. Finally, Robert finished making a car big enough for Mark to ride. Mark climbed in and rode around the front room, through the kitchen and down the hall.

"I'm going to make a jeep now!" Robert said. He started to take the car apart. Mark wailed. He wanted Robert's Christmas present.

Maybe I should have given an *Erector* set to each boy, so that Mark could ride while Robert rebuilds a second one.

Credits: vertical stripes paper by Memory Press, dark denim paper by Hot Off The Press, light denim paper by Geographics, die cuts by Ellison, (nuts & bolts handmade), paper crimper, stamp and zipper paper edgers by Fiskars®, mini-extension diamond punch by Family Treasures

Page Layout Tips

You should be having fun with your layouts. If it has become a chore, then it's time to simplify your pages.

Die cuts are a quick and easy way to "jazz up" your pages. There is a wide assortment of precut shapes and sizes at most scrapbooking stores.

Note: Paper crimpers add variety and dimension to you your layouts.

Writing Tips

Tell about your child's first steps. How long did he crawl? Was your child brave, foolhardy or hesitant? Where were his first steps taken? Re-create the moment.

Use Dialogue

Writing dialogue is important in making your photographs come to life. Capture your child's actions and words and you will have found your best writing. Note that children say short sentences with only a few simple words. Use the words and comments that represent them best.

Children are always coming up with fresh ways of looking at life. Listen to your child when he speaks. Can you capture one of your child's favorite expressions? Try writing one down. If you don't, what he says will be forgotten.

When you write dialogue, don't use long words or long descriptive sentences unless that's the way the child ordinarily speaks. Let his words sound natural.

If a child has a favorite word, use it. Slang comes and goes, but it's fun to record. When I was a girl, "hubba! hubba!" was what you said when you saw someone you liked. It dates your writing when you use slang, but it is also a colorful part of history. I gave my grandson a video tape for Christmas, and his comment was, "That's tight," which his mother interpreted as an "acceptable" gift.

If I were to present the story on this page without dialogue, it would read something like this: Today I taught Mark's 3-year-old Junior Sunday School class. The lesson was on "Things that are good for our body." All of the children tried to participate, but I'm not sure that they understood the concept of good food. Russell was obsessed with his dog and that it liked to drink water with flies in it. Mark must have been hungry, and Blake's mother is going to have a baby. I don't think anyone listened to anyone except himself.

Compare the writing and you can see that with dialogue you can show the child and the situation far better than if you just tell the story.

JULY 1966

DOGGIE

MILK

Today I taught Mark's 3-year-old Junior Sunday School class. The lesson was on "Things that are good for our body." This is how it went...

Me: What are good things we all like to drink?
Mark: I like watermelon.
Me: How many of you drink water?
Russell: My dog likes water, only there's flies in his water.
Me: We all like nice clean water. It makes us grow.
Russell: My dog likes to drink flies.
Me: How many of you boys drank a nice glass of milk before you came?
Blake: My mama's going to have a baby.
Me: Your baby will like to drink milk.
Mark: I like root beer.
Russell: My dog likes root beer...with flies.
Blake: My grandma's coming today.
Russell: Teacher...guess what my dog likes to drink?

Page Layout Tips

Many acid-free stickers are now available. These may be used as borders or to accent your pages. Check to see if the stickers you are using are photo safe.

Use stickers like spice. If you put too many on one page, your layouts may give you heartburn.

Use your stickers in the proper setting and coordinate them with your page layout theme. It may not be appropriate to use stickers on an heirloom page.

Credits: linen paper by Memory Press, red honey checks paper by Provo Craft, stickers by DMD Industries, Inc., pinking paper edgers and art deco corner edgers by Fiskars®.

Writing Tips

Your child has his own way of expressing himself. He uses a favorite word or words all the time. Capture them and use them in stories or Quick-tell phrases on your layout pages.

Try Writing Humor

Don't preface your story by saying that you are going to tell something funny. When you say, "Let me tell you a funny joke," you are setting yourself up to fail. At that moment, you must prove that your joke is funny. Start at the beginning without a challenge.

Don't explain the joke. There is always someone who wants to go back and try to explain. If I had finished the story about Greg and Uncle Roy and then tried to explain that in opera everything is sung, and that Greg was trying to improve the whole opera system, then I would have ruined the entire story.

Exaggeration is a natural part of humor, but keep it to a minimum. If you have a story that you think is funny, tell it as it is. Present the story in a logical order. Then give the punch line. Some stories are smiling funny, others are wry-grin funny and a few are laugh-out-loud funny. Remember, this is your child's history. If you try too hard to be funny, you may sacrifice the truth.

Give a background to your story, build, then stop. Outline your humor, either in your mind or on paper. When you start, give your reader all the needed background information. You know what the punch line is, so make sure that necessary details have been included before you get there. There is nothing worse than to get to the punch line and then have to say, "Oh, yes, I forgot to tell you..." Develop your story, building idea upon idea. Work toward your punch line. Give the funny line. Then stop.

Place your punch line last. The most important line in a humorous story is the last line, with the last word receiving the most emphasis. Work with your story until you get it right. For the greatest impact, try to make your last word your strongest.

Last Wednesday we took five-year-old Greg to the opera, *Falstaff*, where Uncle Roy sang the lead. As usual Roy did a magnificent job, but toward the end of the opera Greg got squirmy. We went backstage afterwards and Greg asked him, "Don't you get tired of singing everything? Why don't you just say the words?"
March 1991

Credits: stationery by Action Papers, die cuts by Ellison, Victorian paper edgers by Fiskars®, pen by Uchida

Page Layout Tips

Use scrapbooking materials and tools that reflect your theme. For instance, on this page, we wanted to evoke a classy feeling. Notice that the stationery, die cuts, photograph, paper edgers and even the choice of colors all tie into "a night at the opera."

Writing Tips

Not every funny story ends with a punch line. Tell it as it happened. Sometimes words weren't used, but the actions were humorous. Without trying to be funny, take each pertinent action and show how it snowballs.

Show a Few Bugs on Your Roses

This story about report cards can be enjoyable to your child in years to come, even if he doesn't appreciate it now. Not everything in the child's life is going to be perfect. My children went through difficult times in school and were often troublesome and obnoxious.

You aren't going to want to show the child being cruel, malicious, or truly bad, but if you always show him as perfect, he is going to know that what you have written in his book isn't honest.

Round out your stories by adding prankish things your child has done. These stories are fun to write and show his personality. Sometimes it is refreshing to show your child with a little mischief in his heart. Is there any child who hasn't checked out the Christmas presents hidden in the closet? Most kids will squeeze a present, shake it, smell it, and try in any way possible to guess the gift. One of my children unwrapped every one of his gifts, checked them out, and then wrapped them up again. He did this every year and I didn't know what he had done until he was grown.

I was less than perfect too. My grandmother always kept candy in her upper bureau drawer under some handkerchiefs. I admit to snitching more than my share.

My grand-daughter found out that she could get her brothers in trouble by going into the bathroom and putting up the toilet seat. Her mom scolded the boys about forgetting to put the seat down, and the boys protested that they had remembered. My grand-daughter had so much fun, but she tried the trick once too often and got caught.

This story shows my grand-daughter's personality better than if I had told about her getting A's in school, or that she keeps a tidy room.

The Report Card

Nov. 1995

The children's report cards came home this evening. They are not as good as they should be, I'm afraid. Tom came in fuming and fussing.

"Name all the bad things in the world, mother," he said. "That's what my teacher is."

Tomorrow is teacher appreciation day and each child in the school is supposed to take a home-made card to his teacher. Tom couldn't find enough horrible things so he finally settled on a modern art picture of his own creation, and I hope that his teacher doesn't understand modern art. By this evening he had calmed down somewhat and didn't refer to her as a slimy snake or a lizard and she had advanced up the scale to the insect world.

Used with permission of MM's Designs

Credits: stationery by MM's Designs, bow tie paper edgers by Fiskars®, deckle edge scissors by Family Treasures

Page Layout Tips

Try to balance your photos and stories on the page. Heavier and larger items usually look better on the bottom half.

Don't be afraid to angle and overlap your photos. Move things around until they are pleasing to the eye.

Writing Tips

This one page may change your whole outlook on life. When your child is being obnoxious, troublesome, or mischievous, look at his behavior as a great "writing opportunity."

I stopped watching Bill ski when he graduated from the bunny hill. That was several years ago. Now when he comes home he tells me all about taking the jumps.

"Come watch me," he begged.

"Watch you crash over some cliff! No way!"

The next time he went skiing he hired a photographer to video him on the jumps. The video showed him jumping off cliffs and even though I knew it was staged for my benefit, I marveled at what he could do. I don't know where he got such grace and courage.

Go Big!

Spread Eagle

Alta Utah Area Trail Map

Chad Grennan & Bill Dixon Winter 89/90

www.real pain.com

Decorative Designs© & ™Ellison
Licensed Product

Credits: paper by The Paper Patch, die cuts by Ellison, stickers by Stickopotamus, deckle edge scissors by Family Treasures, pen by Uchida

Brag a Bit

As you write, keep your stories upbeat. Make sure that the tone of your writing is not one of criticism, but one of praise. Remember that your child will go back and read what you have written, especially when you brag a bit.

Tell about an achievement or character trait your child has. Find a good example to illustrate that quality and summarize in detail about the success your child may achieve if he continues in this endeavor. Make sure you write honestly. If you overdo your plaudits, the child may think you are making fun of him.

Writing Tips

Look for ways you can compliment your child. Write a note of appreciation and put it on his pillow or place it on the refrigerator. The note doesn't have to be great. A simple statement will do, "Thank you, Scott, for taking out the trash today. I love you. Mom."

After these notes have been enjoyed, save them in his file to be used in his scrapbook.

Page Layout Tips

Many people like to follow a theme. Lay out your stories and photos and decide their placement before you adhere them.

Let the photos follow a progression of action, just as a story proceeds in logical sequence. The first page should introduce the next few pages of photos.

Does your child take swimming lessons, play soccer, write poetry, draw pictures (by the bushel), or stand on his head? All of these are possible bragging moments.

But don't forget the day after day monotonous times he did his chores without prodding or acted responsibly with his paper route. Remember the time he made breakfast for you? Never mind the mess. It was the thought that counted.

One objective in scrapbooking is to bring your child back to his scrapbook to read and re-read. Every time you brag, your child knows that you love him. He will know that you mean what you say, because you took the time to write about his accomplishments.

Daniel's Artwork
Age 8

Yesterday, Daniel went on a field trip to a dairy. He's been studying cows and brought home a picture that he had drawn. "That's its stomach," he told me pointing to his masterpiece. "It eats grass, then burps it back to stomach 2, then burps it back to stomach 3, then burps it to stomach 4, and then burps it into milk." And to think we've been drinking milk all these years...and liking it!

May 1967

Pictures Children Draw

We all have them—pictures the children have drawn. At first it is exciting to see button-eyed stick figures, but after awhile, you wonder where you will put them all. Before you file a drawing, sit down with your child and ask him to tell about the picture. When you write down a few of the child's ideas about his artwork, you have a record of how he thinks as well as what he has drawn. It seems that my children showed me their drawings when I was busy, so I only jotted the main idea. If I found the story and artwork interesting, I wrote in more detail later.

Sometimes the story the child tells makes his drawings memorable. This is what I did with the cow story. I simply wrote down Dan's explanation.

Some pictures are better than others just as some stories are better. Your scrapbook can hold only so many drawings, so you must be selective. Save the pictures, but include only the best in his scrapbook, along with the story he tells you. The others can be placed in dated envelopes, files or binders. Why not present excess drawings as a wedding gift when your child marries?

If you're working with old drawings, don't sacrifice the memory for a perfect layout. This cow picture was too big to fit vertically in a scrapbook so it was turned and the ragged edges trimmed slightly. Dan's children giggle at his comments and drawing 30 years later.

Writing Tips

Ask your child to draw a picture of a friend he would like to have. When he has finished the picture, ask him questions about what he and his friend might like to do together. Follow him in his imagination and write his story as he tells it. You can both have fun together.

Credits: deckle edge scissors by Family Treasures, cow punch by Uchida, drawing and scientific explanation by Dan Dixon

Page Layout Tips

You can use the child's drawings as background pages in his scrapbook or cut out smaller drawings to use as page decorations.

However, if the drawing has been colored with crayons or is on paper from school, it may not be photo safe. Have the artwork color copied for his scrapbook and then save the originals in a folder or box away from your photos.

My Daddy bring me a grasshopper My grasshopper jumps on the rug. No, no, Wobert. Don't eat my grasshopper. My put my grasshopper in bottle. My grasshopper eats grass. My give my grasshopper more grass. Where my grasshopper? No, no, Wobert. Don't eat my grasshopper. No, no, Wobert! My grasshopper - all gone.
(by Charles Dixon, age 3, August 9, 1958)

Credits: clip art, crayon font and design layout by DJ Inkers

Writing Tips

For a time, my son had an imaginary friend whom he called his "workman." Many times, he told me about their adventures together. Stories like these are fun to capture on paper. When I tell my son about his whimsical friend now, he doesn't believe me. But I wrote down some of his "workman" stories, so I have proof.

Page Layout Tips

When you cut around a person in a photograph and place it on your layout, the figure can sometimes appear to be floating. Grounding your figure on a base will help avoid this problem. The figure can be at the bottom of your layout or on an object. In this layout the children have been grounded by placing them on a swing.

Stories Children Tell

A sample of the child's writing is fun to include. You can let it stand by itself or add your own comments.

Charles was only three years old, but even then he was fascinated by insects. As I stood watching him, he started talking to his baby brother. I wrote down most of what he said, (language uncorrected) and included it in a family letter about 40 years ago.

Back then, I found that children love to write stories if they don't have to be bothered with the mechanics. This understanding came when I taught a class on Creative Writing for children. The children wrote a story and drew an illustration. (Sometimes the illustration came first and then the story.) I talked to each child about a story he wanted to write. I asked him questions and after we had discussed it for a while, I got out my typewriter and wrote while the child dictated. This way, the child didn't have to worry about the mechanics of writing.

Afterwards, I read the story back to the child and asked if that was what he wanted to say.

One boy had had a traumatic experience the day before. He had been to a aviary and had watched one rooster attack another smaller rooster in the cage. The boy started telling the story and I typed as fast as the boy talked. He told how helpless he felt being on the other side of the cage and not being able to stop the fight. He had tried desperately to find someone to help the rooster, but there was no one.

The story became bigger than just a rooster fight. It became a symbol of all the injustices in the world.

Children do know about life and may express it in their writing. Talk to them about the story they want to create. Write it down. Let them know that you will help them, but that the story belongs to them.

Credits: background texture paper by Close to My Heart™, peak paper edgers by Fiskars®, markers by Tombow®, star template by Creative Memories, layout by D.O.T.S Design Studio

Used with the permission of Suzy's Zoo® San Diego, CA (619) 452-9401

Decorative Designs© & ™Ellison. Licensed Product

Notes Children Write

Be sure to include notes and letters written in the child's own handwriting. These can be assignments written at school, notes, or "thank you's" from your child.

Children are often asked to write short essays. Save the best for your child's scrapbook. The example on the above left is a school assignment written by Dan for Mother's Day. I still get thanks from Dan, but the times when he was young are now gone. I'm glad that I saved this wonderful note from my son. I'm also encouraged that I fed him right.

On the above right is a list of things Crisy wanted to accomplish one day. Interpreted: Put shoes on, get dressed, eat breakfast, get backpack, go to school, learn. Crisy's spelling is much better now, but for a short time in her life, she was a creative speller.

You might get in the habit of writing to each other and leaving it in a special book or in a note hung by magnets on the refrigerator. These notes can be fun for both of you. Some might be fun enough for a scrapbook.

These times go by so quickly. Catch a few of the reminders of their childhood while you can.

Page Layout Tips

Use a ruler or paper cutter to get nice, clean edges on your photos and papers.

If cutting in a straight line is a problem for you, use a deckle style scissor/edger. The deckle design is great for covering up slightly crooked edges.

Writing Tips

Set up an area or container with supplies available for your child. Include writing and art papers, scissors, paper, glue, colored pencils, and rulers. If a child knows where to go for supplies, she will be more inclined to write or draw.

Credits: (Things I gotta do) paper by The Paper Patch, notepaper by Suzy's Zoo, push pin die cut by Ellison, grass die cut by Pebbles in my Pocket

The Art of Writing Scrapbook Stories©

The Dixon Family
1934

Back row: Willard
True (mother)
Charles (father)
Front row: Elaine
Jean & June (twins)

True and Willard 1998

My mother-in-law, who is now 95 years old, tells about my husband when he was in first grade.

Mother reminisced, "Willard refused to work for his teacher, He would ask me, 'Why does my teacher look like a gorilla and why are her teeth so yellow?' Then he brushed his teeth until his gums bled."

"What happened then?" I asked.

Mother drew in her breath and declared, "Well, Charles went straight to the Superintendent of Schools and had Willard moved to another class. After that, Willard loved school."

"And did his teacher look like a gorilla?" I asked. Mother looked up at Willard and grinned.

It's Not Too Late

Throughout this book I have said, "Write your child's stories before you forget." I'm not rescinding that advice but am adding to it. It is never too late to write about your older children, your spouse or your own stories. (See example left)

Your older children enjoy having their photos displayed and their stories told. Even if you haven't written about them before, you can still start. You have plenty of their photos. Now their stories need to be remembered. You don't need to write about each photo, but you can remember things your older child has said and done. As memory jogs you, write it down. Find a photo to match the time frame and you already have a good start.

The older child's scrapbook may not be as long or as involved as the preschooler or elementary age child, but the stories you remember will be as important to that child as it is to the youngster.

If you are working on your own scrapbook or another adult family member's book, make sure your/their stories are recorded as well. Write down the stories your parents and grandparents have told. Family stories, written one at a time, are the beginning of a family history. Try to locate a photo to accompany the story. A few layouts with photos and remembrances will make a family history come to life for you, your children, and generations to follow.

Scrapbooking is for everyone. Photograph albums are no longer pages of unsmiling, silent people. They are vivacious people with plenty to say, and lots of life still in them. With your exciting ideas, their words and pictures, you can create a bridge from generation to generation.

For more in-depth information on this subject, read my book, **Family Focused, a step-by-step guide to writing your autobiography and family history.**

Writing Tips

What happens in the world also affects your child. Too many times we never mention floods, severe snow storms, war, death of a favorite hero, or politics in a child's scrapbook, but history shapes each person's life and should be mentioned.

Photo copy a pertinent current headline that affects your child. In the years to come, this event will be history, and your child will have experienced it.

Credits: paper by Hot Off The Press, template die cut by Accu-Cut Systems®, pen by Zig Memory System® Writer

Page Layout Tips

If you don't have a lot of time to spend on your layout, use a precut template. It is easy to slide a story as well as a photo under a template opening.

Don't hand color tint an old photograph. Instead, have a copy made and work from that.

Archival Tips

There are many types of Archival Preservationists:

Purist: Those who create a book that would last forever in a dark, cold tomb, never to be read or touched.

Less than Purist: Those who create a book to last only 300 years. These LTP's read every research and archival publication before buying a glue stick.

Scrapbooker: Those who create a book to last a mere 75 years. These brilliant artists use photo safe products and allow their work to be handled by slightly unsterile little fingers.

Purist Rebel: Those who leave photos and mementos in rat-chewed, acid-ridden shoe boxes.

Choose quality products that have been tested and proven to be photo safe. If you're not sure, check with the manufacturer. They are usually happy to assist you.

Photographs

Take your photographs out of the shoe boxes and dresser drawers and sort them. Store them in acid-free boxes, folders or files. If you have photographs that are irreplaceable, get a copy made. There are three ways you can do this:

1. Get the photo copied at a qualified photography shop. These copies are more expensive, but once you have a negative made, you can make as many duplicates as you want for each family member. These may be photographs of grandparents, ancestors, or even special photos of the child. If you have a studio portrait made, remember that the studio has the copyright and you have to get a release to make copies. Older portrait photos are not copyrighted

2. Have a color copy made at a copy center. Some places will copy for under a dollar and these are fine for most scrapbooks, especially those that are going to be handled by younger children.

3. Scan the photo into your computer. Scanners are becoming less expensive and easier to use all the time.

Note: Photo-tinting is becoming more and more popular. If you decide to photo-tint an old black and white photograph, color the copy, not the original.

Binders

There are many binders on the market today. The most expensive will be acid-free with a dust cover. Avoid vinyl binders as they are harmful to your photographs. More companies are producing quality archival binders, especially those associated with the **Binding Industries of America Association**. Three-ringed binders with "D" shaped rings are easy to use because sheet protectors and paper can easily be found to fit. Another option is to use screw post or post bound binders. There are many variations of the post bound binder. One of their advantages is that they do not come apart easily if dropped. Creative Memories uses a flex-hinge™ binding system which allows the book to always lie flat even when you add more pages. Their binder uses a larger size paper.

Protective Sheets

You can compose your layout pages and slip them into the protective polypropylene, polyethylene or mylar sheets. Now your child can look at her pictures as much as she wants and the oil and dirt from her fingers will not destroy her photos. Stay away from magnetic sheets. Even if these companies say their products are acid-free, you still have the adhesive backing with which to be concerned.

Papers

Whether you use brightly colored cardstock, or patterned background paper on which to mount your photographs, try to ensure that your materials are acid-free, lignin-free and buffered to prevent damage to your photographs. Many scrapbook supply stores are now carrying an assortment of photo safe papers. You may also use these papers for punches and die cuts. Test your paper for acid content using a pH testing pen.

Adhesives

When you adhere photos to paper, you must be able to reverse the process; this is one of the first rules of archival preservation. Never glue or tape photos back to back. Do your layouts on separate sheets of paper and then they may be placed (not glued) back to back in a sheet protector. Many adhesives on the market will damage photos. Make sure the product you are using has been approved as an archival product. I use double-sided photo splits or tape because they are easy to use and not messy. Photo corners are another option. Some people like glue sticks because they are quick. Glue sticks may be used on photos and larger pieces of artwork. On smaller artwork, you will have better control using an acid-free, xylene-free glue pen, such as the Zig® 2-Way Glue.

Pens and Pencils

Graphite pencils are safe to use on the back of old photographs for identification. (Never use ball point pens.) Acid-free permanent pigment ink pens that don't fade, bleed or stain are available and may be used on your page layouts. Archivally approved colored pencils and markers may also be used to decorate your pages. Red-eye pens can be used to cover up red-eye problems in photographs.

Decorative aids

Decorative aids such as die cuts, craft punches, patterned scissors/edgers, stencils, templates, stamps, and stickers, can be used to enhance your layout pages.

Memorabilia may also be added to your scrapbooks, such as tickets, postcards, programs, maps, certificates etc. You may need to deacidify these first.

Note from the Author

Has your child said the most unforgettable things lately? You have already told your husband, your mother, mother-law, best friend, neighbor and then maybe even started a second re-telling. "You told us already," they might have said.

But have you written it down? Because, you see, your child is going to give another clever witticism and you are going to start the round again, and maybe the first "unforgettable saying" will be forgotten. Yes, it is possible to forget!

This is how I started writing the stories that are in this book. I exhausted all my close friends and relatives and then extended my stories to relatives far away. Because, you see, my children's sayings could not be confined within my geographic area, they had to be sent by mail. I wrote my letters making sure each child had a paragraph or two with his sayings and doings.

Even this wasn't good enough. I made two copies of my letter, and saved one in its entirety. I cut up the second copy and put a paragraph in each child's scrapbook.

After awhile, I noticed that the children were getting out their scrapbooks, reading what I had said about them, and then telling the stories to their friends. They hadn't realized how witty they were when they were little. But Mama had known all along that each child was brilliant.

Writing letters had added benefits, too. My neighbors stopped running when I came around. They didn't always have something burning on the stove whenever I started telling about my precocious children. Because, instead of telling my stories several times, I was writing them down in my letters. So, if your child says something hilarious, thoughtful, or insightful write a letter.

Janice T. Dixon, Ph.D.

Janice Dixon is an award-winning writer and educator. She wrote **Family Focused**, published by Mount Olympus Publishing, and **Preserving Your Past**, with Dora Flack, published by Doubleday. Dr. Dixon has taught classes in personal and family history at the Brigham Young University. She shared many of her secrets at the **World Conference of Records** in 1980 and has continued offering her valuable and exciting insights in seminars throughout the United States. She has published articles and stories and has had twelve of her plays produced. She is the mother of six children and 17 grandchildren.

Send Us Your Best Story on a Layout Page

Send us a color copy of your best story on a layout page and it may be included in one of our next books. Be sure to include a list of all products used including paper, die cuts, craft punches, scissors/edgers, stickers, templates, tools, rulers, stamps, pens, pencils, markers, computer programs, clip art, fonts, etc. so that we can get written permission from the manufacturers. Layouts will be chosen based on quality and those that best fit our needs.

Stories to consider include:

    Younger children
    Older children (teenagers or grown children)
    Autobiographical stories
    Parents/Grandparents
    Adopted family members
    Other family members
    Pets

Your name, address, telephone number and mailing date should be on all items. Unused contributions cannot be acknowledged or returned. Please send submissions to P.O. Box 65966, Salt Lake City, Utah 84165-0966

Let Us Know

How has **The Art of Writing Scrapbook Stories©** helped you? Please send comments telling us how this book assisted you in your writing and page layouts.

We would also like to improve future books. Send your suggestions to the address listed on the left. Your feedback will be greatly appreciated.

Lucy is getting excited about going to school for the first time. She puts all of her dolls in a row to teach them. Sometimes Mark gets included and he is a model student.

Of course, if he isn't, she pops him one...he pops her back...and Lucy declares a recess.
July 1966

children, © Ellison

SCHOOL BUS

bus, Pebbles in my Pocket

© Ellison

The Art of Writing Scrapbook Stories© will inspire you to write about your child. This remarkable book has warmth, humor and valuable suggestions to help you get started whether your child is three, thirteen, or thirty-three. In fact, with the author's help, you'll not only be **able** to write your treasured stories, you'll find that you **want** to write them.

This book includes:

1. Simplified writing instructions in easy, enjoyable steps
2. Fun to read illustrative stories
3. "Make-it-easy" writing tips
4. Page layout tips
5. Archival tips
6. Full color examples showing how stories, photographs and scrapbooking products can be combined to make scrapbooks attractive and fun to read.

January 10, 1995

Dear James,
This is a picture Ben drew for you. It is a picture of a beautiful girl. Now that you will be home soon, you can start looking for a girl to marry who looks like this. ♥
Love, Mom

ISBN 0-9656919-7-0

5119

9 780965 691970